Moving Beyond
Adultery and Divorce

by **Corinne Burdett**

Monterey Pacific Publishing

ISBN 1-889710-37-4

Monterey Pacific Publishing

Printed in Canada

This book is lovingly dedicated to my parents
who taught me to value life and care about people
and to my fantastic kids
who have always been there for me.

Acknowledgement

I thank God for guiding and sustaining me,
especially through this difficult time in my life.
I also wish to thank all my family and friends
for their continued love and support.

Contents

CHAPTER ONE
Our Marriage

October 5, 1990..... That day I discovered the affair and my life changed forever! I can't begin to explain the pain and horror I felt when I found out that Mike, the man I had loved since I was 17 years old, was being unfaithful to me. I honestly never suspected it. I had really believed that all the changes and stress in him were job related. It was an accident that day, when I opened his briefcase to put some mail inside and found evidence of his adultery. I was in disbelief and tried to rationalize the hotel and limousine receipts in my hand.

No, I didn't want to believe it. As I look back, I can see why I was in such shock. We were a successful, happy (or so I thought), "baby boomer" couple. Life had been good to us. I assumed that we both took our marriage vows seriously. To me, marriage meant a sacred covenant between two people. I believed it meant the same to Mike.

Because of my background and beliefs, I wanted my marriage to be forever. In my thinking, divorce would never be an option.

I had known Mike since high school. We had been in several classes together and I was drawn to his flamboyant personality. We had started dating in our senior year, and by the end of that summer, we were talking seriously about a future together. In the fall I went away to a two-year college for women while Mike attended a business school at home. We visited each other often during that first year and kept our relationship very much alive. We were young and in love.

Falling in love was wonderful, but my emotions and excitement kept me from seeing Mike realistically. Even when I finally did begin to notice his faults, I chose to ignore them because I was so in love. I witnessed Mike's explosive temper on many occasions. Everyone would make excuses for him and I found myself doing the same thing. Mike was also very opinionated. He seemed to think that he was always right and that others' thoughts and ideas were wrong. He would go to great lengths to make sure that I agreed with him. I should have paid more attention to this side of Mike, but I was caught up in his outgoing, fun personality. In many ways we were very different, and that made him more attractive to me.

Mike also got to witness some of my faults. He just couldn't believe how stubborn and impatient I could be. Once I set my mind on something, it was hard to get me to change. Also, my impatient personality had gotten me into all sorts of trouble and gained me the reputation of being "ditsy." Mike also knew that I was accident prone, especially when it came to driving. Many of my escapades and accidents had been quite costly. But in spite of everything, we continued to date and to fall madly in love with one another.

During my second year of college, Mike joined the Army Reserves and went off to basic training. He was gone for six months, although it seemed much longer. The time apart proved to be worth it since the reserves ultimately kept Mike from ever having to fight in the Vietnam War.

When he returned from basic training, we became engaged; eight months later, we were married.

During our first year of marriage our daughter, Jennifer, was born. We had some tough times financially, but Mike had decided that he did not want me to work outside the home. I was very content being a homemaker and raising our daughter. Even when we faced difficulties, it seemed that we both felt our love for one another would be enough to see us through.

We bought our first house after we'd been married two years. The following year our first son, Richard, was born. We were so excited. We had two healthy children, a nice home, and each other. Life was good and we were happy.

Growing up, Mike and I had attended church. We both decided that it was time for us to become involved with a church and go regularly for the sake of our children.

As I thought about my spirituality, I became confused about the place religion played in my life. I contemplated the purpose of my existence and worried about my eternal destiny. I wondered, "Where will I go when I die?" or, "How will God decide if I am good enough to enter heaven?" I had no answers for these questions. I did believe in God and His son Jesus, but wondered how they fit into my life. I set out on a journey trying to secure my own eternal destiny. I struggled to be good enough so that God would accept me. I did all kinds of volunteer work and became very active in our church. As a result of all my efforts, all I got was tired out and exhausted. I found it impossible to live this way all the time and soon realized that there had to be another way. But I wondered what it could be?

At this time Mike was offered a job in upstate New York. Because of all the advantages, we decided to make the move. Once again, I thought I'd try religious and volunteer activities in my pursuit of personal fulfillment.

My new neighbor told me about a local Christian Women's Club. It sounded interesting to me, so I made a reservation for their monthly luncheon.

On September 8, 1975, I attended the luncheon all by myself. The women were friendly and seemed to be having a good time, so I relaxed and enjoyed the afternoon. The program included a fashion show and special speaker. I was anxious to hear what this speaker would have to say. She seemed to be a woman much like myself. She had put her career on hold in order to raise her children. She looked about my age. As she proceeded to tell us about her own life story, I listened intently.

After she talked about her early life, she told us about an internal emptiness that she had felt most of her life. She had tried to fill the empty hole with her family and material objects. Boy, could I relate to that since I was doing the same thing. She explained how she tried to please God and to earn His acceptance by being good. She had my attention now. She had done all kinds of volunteer work, gone to church, and struggled daily to be a good person. I thought to myself, "She **is** exactly like me."

Then she declared that if she had died at that time in her life, she would not have gone to heaven. Did that mean I wouldn't either? Now I was concerned and listening to every word she said.

She read from her Bible where Jesus said, "I am the way, the truth and the life; no one comes to the Father but through me" (John 3:16). She continued reading from the Bible, "But God showed His great love for us by sending Christ to die for us while we were still sinners." I didn't have to try to be good for God to accept me. In fact, God said, "And all our righteous deeds are like a filthy garment..." (Is. 64:6).

She then told us how she had accepted Jesus Christ as her Savior and had found her fulfillment in Him. I understood for the first time that His gift of eternal life is free; and I had insulted him by trying to earn it. I realized I just needed to reach out and accept God's gift. For the first time in my life, it became clear to me that good works and religion would not meet my needs; only Christ himself could do that. He alone could bring purpose and fulfillment to my life.

At the end of her message she led in a prayer, and I asked God to forgive my sins and to come into my life as Savior and

Lord. I left the luncheon that day with my questions finally answered and a peace in my heart that I had never felt before.

Within a few weeks, I was attending a Friendship Bible Coffee and learning how to apply the Bible to my daily life. As I read the Bible, God showed me that I needed to yield my stubbornness and impatience to Him. He didn't want to change my personality completely, but He did want to get it under His control. So as I began changing, Mike became curious.

It wasn't long until I was very involved in the Christian Women's Club myself. I made several new friends there. One of them invited Mike and me to attend a Bible Study which she and her husband were going to host in their home. I got excited in hopes that Mike would go with me. But when I mentioned it to him, his answer was, "No." He said that he did not want to spend his Friday evenings studying the Bible. I didn't say anything more to him about it. A few weeks later when he saw that I was not attending without him, he said unexpectedly that he would go with me . . . but just once. He seemed surprised when he met the men. They were successful and down to earth—not the wimps he thought they would be. They even liked to play golf. He felt comfortable with them and decided to go every week. After about eight months of studying, listening and asking questions, Mike got alone with God and accepted Christ into his life.

I immediately began to see changes in Mike as he yielded himself to God. His quick temper and sudden outbursts began to disappear. He became less and less opinionated as he listened to my ideas and began to trust my judgment. He was more sympathetic as he developed a heart for people and their needs. His angry spirit was replaced with a tenderness I'd not seen in him before.

As new Christians, we wanted to continue our growth; thus, we became involved in a small church in our new area.

We both felt comfortable and accepted in our new environment. Within a year, we were asked to be the youth leaders. Mike's charismatic personality drew the young people to him. We both found that guiding teens in their spiritual walk was not only fulfilling but fun. Besides our weekly Bible Studies, we had retreats, hayrides, slumber parties and gatherings in our home where the kids felt comfortable talking with us about their personal lives and problems. We were really enjoying our new life as Christians.

Life did seem good and we were very happy. Our love for each other flourished as we followed after God and served him side by side. We were then blessed with the birth of our second son, Donald. I experienced complications, and Don was born three weeks prematurely. Consequently, he had some problems with his lungs, and at three months old, he was put into the hospital with pneumonia. His right lung collapsed and he came very close to death. This drove us deeper into our Christian walk as we prayed for our new son. Don survived, but for years struggled with pneumonia and croup.

Because of Don's health and Mike's discontentment with his job, we decided to pursue a move west to a warmer and drier climate. The friends who had hosted the couples' Bible Study which we had attended now lived in Arizona. We went to visit them and to check out the area as a possibility for our move. The husband, Jim, had been involved in an affair and was once again living at home. We had hopes that they could restore their marriage and we wanted to do whatever we could to help. It was an uncomfortable visit for us both. Jim acted as if he did not want to be there. The whole atmosphere of the home was tense. Soon after our visit, we learned that Jim had left his family again and had returned to the other woman. Mike was shocked. He couldn't believe that Jim would leave his wife and family. Mike gathered the men from the old Bible Study together to pray for Jim. Seeing Mike's horror and shock over this situation gave me a secure feeling that this was something he would never let happen to us.

While we were still seeking to make a move, Fred, an old friend of Mike's, called and offered him a job with his company in California. Fred was the company's Vice President of Finance. He was looking to hire a Controller for his company. I was not eager to move to California because I feared the earthquakes, but God reminded me in His quiet way that He could protect me anywhere.

So in 1980, we moved to San Jose. Mike moved in February, three months ahead of the rest of the family. I stayed behind in New York to sell the house and arrange for the movers. Except for the six months we had been apart when Mike was in basic training, we had never been separated for more than a few days. I was very lonely and missed him a lot. I was overwhelmed with all that I had to do to prepare for this move. I was also a little resentful that he had dumped the responsibility of the move and sale of our home all on me. He was enjoying California and the sunshine while I was stuck in snowy, cold upstate New York.

While Mike was in San Jose alone, he began searching for a church. He quickly found one that he liked and he began to attend regularly. He and Ron, the Pastor, became friends. By the time the kids and I finally arrived in May, we had a church family and friends to welcome us. Ron and his wife, Joyce, gave us friendship and spiritual guidance. It was comforting to have such wonderful support so soon.

Several months later at work, Mike learned that Fred was to be fired. Mike was shocked. We both worried about what the company would now do with Mike since Fred had been the one to hire him. Very soon our worry turned to surprise as Mike was promoted into Fred's position as Vice President of Finance. It was a miracle. Mike had never even gotten his college degree, and here he was a Vice President. We truly saw

God's hand on his life. He used his new position as an avenue to share Christ with other businessmen. He was dedicated to his job and to serving his God.

Mike became more active in church as he attended a weekly men's prayer meeting, led a Bible Study in our home, and worked with the single adults. He was busy stretching his time between his family, ministry and job.

Our three children also kept us both very busy. We attended all their sporting events and school activities. Home life was important to us, so we tried to spend large amounts of time together. We had many trips to Disneyland, enjoying southern California. One spring, we rented a houseboat on Lake Mead, and in the winter, we rented a mountain cabin. We even splurged and took the kids to Hawaii twice. We just had fun as a family, whatever we did.

Mike and I were getting along very well. Our marriage wasn't perfect, but we worked on it together, using the Bible as our daily guide. We continued to develop a close friendship with Ron and Joyce, and during these years, spent hours playing and working together with them. I truly believe these were our best years as husband and wife. During this time, I felt loved by and special to Mike. I believed I was #1 right under God. Almost every night at bedtime, we shared about our day, laughed, and then prayed together. Afterward we would often make love. I believed that this was God's model for marriage. This was the happiest and most secure time in my life.

As I grew in my Christian walk, God gave me a ministry with women. I taught a Bible Study on, "How to be the Wife of a Happy Husband," by Darian Cooper. I also led women in a study in which I wrote about sex in marriage. I encouraged women to let down their sexual barriers, relax, and enjoy their husbands.

At the same time, I was beginning to have a counseling ministry with women in the church. I felt God leading me more and more in that direction. I was excited because now I had my own ministries.

Suddenly, I began to experience depression and mood swings. My life seemed to turn upside down. My menstrual cycle came to an abrupt halt. I was sure I wasn't pregnant. After Don was born, I had a tubal ligation. My doctor had no answers, so he blamed it all on stress. I knew that was not accurate; this was a peaceful time in my life. Finally, after I had endured months of tears and confusion, my doctor tested my hormones and discovered I was in menopause at only 35 years of age. That was a horrible year for me until I was given ERT (Estrogen Replacement Therapy). After that, I quickly returned to my old self. I appreciated Mike's support and patience during that time.

After that chaotic year, life began to settle down for us again. We did go through some upsets with a rebellious teenage daughter. Jennifer was "anti" almost everything we stood for or which was seen as traditional. This was the 80s and she was caught up in the mod scene . . . black clothes and hair, light almost white make-up, and red, red lips. At times it was hard to cope with her. I particularly remember the Sundays she would make her grand entrance into church, always late, wearing her studded black leather jacket and short tight skirts. She always managed to get everyone's attention. Many nights we were on our way to bed as she was heading out the door with her friends. We had a few rough years, but we did get through them.

Life was not always perfect. We had our ups and downs, but when hard times or problems arose, Mike and I coped and made it through them together. I settled on the idea that I could handle anything with God's help and Mike by my side.

In the mid 1980s, Mike was ordained as a lay minister in our denomination. I was proud of him. He had come a long way in his Christian walk. I was somewhat apprehensive because he already had a lot going on in his life. He had just been promoted at work to Executive Vice President, and was being trained to take over as President. I realized his ordination would bring more responsibilities and ministries, but Mike wanted this so much that I kept my thoughts to myself.

Mike loved the thrill of preaching and had quite the flare for it. He began to preach once a month at Juvenile Hall, the City Mission, and Elmwood Women's Jail. He often preached in our church, as well as in other local churches. He absolutely loved to preach and took every opportunity to do so. Needless to say, his schedule was full.

I was back in college now, working toward my B.A. in Clinical Psychology. I was also Director of Vacation Bible School, Sunday School Director, a Friendship Bible Coffee Area Coordinator, homeroom and team mother, and a constant support to Mike in his job and his ministries. Whenever he preached, I was there at his side. We were both living very full lives.

A few years after his ordination, Mike was promoted to President of his company. Before too long, I began to notice that he was changing. At first, he gave God the credit for his accomplishments, but then I saw him become arrogant and boastful. He spent less and less time with the kids, but blamed it on his job and new responsibilities. I took over most of the parenting, hoping to alleviate some of the stress in his life. He traveled a lot and when he was home he was tired. I did accompany him on many of his business trips just so we could have some time together. We found it almost impossible to get away alone just for fun. We had too many obligations.

Our lives continued like this for a couple of years. From my perspective, it seemed that we were being pulled apart by his job, but I still felt that our love was strong. It just seemed that we didn't have enough time together. Mike was still serving God, but it seemed more out of a sense of duty than desire. His job had now taken over as his first priority. God and family fit in when and if there was time left over.

Then, in 1990, his company began the long process of moving their corporate office from San Jose to Lodi. The various plants are located in the San Joaquin Valley and it made sense to have the main office there also. To make the transition easier for everyone, the company decided to rent an apartment in Lodi. The executives would then have a place to stay when they were in town. About this time, Mike began to spend large amounts of time either traveling or at the company apartment.

Now, I really began to see major changes taking place in Mike. I felt an emotional distance between us. We no longer talked and shared our thoughts, dreams and feelings with one another. We never prayed together. In fact, it seemed he had quit praying at all. He would tell me what he thought I wanted to hear. His indifference and phoniness were painful to me. I often caught him lying to others and wondered if he lied to me, too. I no longer knew anything about our financial situation. He kept all our important records and papers at his office.

He began to pull away from his ministries and his friends, including Ron. Ron, Joyce, Mike and I had all left our old church and we were in the process of starting a new, more contemporary church. Mike used this opportunity to pull away from God.

Instead of helping start the new church, Mike became detached and uninterested. Now he was almost never at home, even on the weekends. When he traveled, he no longer wanted to include me. Instead of calling me every night before bed, he started calling me at dinnertime. He would talk for only a few minutes and then rush me off the phone. When I protested his being gone on the weekends, he became hostile with me. The old temper would flare. He even used the kids to try to convince me that he had to be gone all the time. He asked Jennifer to explain to me that with all his new responsibilities as President, he had to travel a lot. Suddenly he was drinking, swearing, and smoking heavily. These were all behaviors that had not been part of his Christian life. I was confused about what was going on with him. I prayed daily for him, as I knew it was hard to be a Christian man in the corporate business world. I put all the blame on the pressures of his job.

Then he made some feeble excuse to change and unlist our telephone number. I noticed his clothes and belongings slowly disappearing from our closet. He was taking them to the Lodi apartment. When I questioned him about it, he told me he'd be working there more often during the transition. So I watched him pulling out of my life and I didn't know what to do.

I became desperate and tried to hang onto my marriage. My demands for his time only pushed him farther away. When he was home, he would lose his temper with me. He blamed me for our problems. He used to be proud that he had a wife who loved God; now he complained about my Christian behavior. The rules had all changed and no one had bothered to tell me.

There was a major part of his life from which I was now excluded. I didn't even know who he was anymore. I really thought it was the pressure of his job, so I began to pray for him to lose his job. I was in a state of panic, wanting to hold onto what we had and yet having to watch it slip away.

The signs were all there, but somehow I had missed them. I had overlooked them because of my image of Mike and also out of my need to protect myself. I soon realized he wasn't changing because of his job, but because he was involved in adultery. That's when I discovered the hotel and limousine receipts and my nightmare began.

CHAPTER TWO
The Affair

After I found the receipts, I couldn't wait to confront Mike. I was hoping for some logical explanation, but in my heart I knew the truth. At first, he denied that he was involved with anyone else. After realizing he was caught, he admitted he'd been seeing Melinda for six months. She lived in Detroit and he was introduced to her when he was there on business. Agony engulfed me as he told me that he loved Melinda and would not give her up. I could not believe what I was hearing. How could this be? How had I missed it? I was overwhelmed and lost control of my emotions. I cried harder and longer than I had ever cried in my life. Grief, fear and anger flooded over me, but I still said that I could forgive him if he would just end it.

We spent the entire night talking. I asked questions that he struggled to answer. Most of all I wanted to know why. The confusion of the previous six months began to make sense to me. No wonder he was never home and I was no longer included on his trips. He was traveling with her. They even had planned a trip to Europe. He had changed our phone number because of her. He was hostile, critical, and blaming of me to justify his own actions. He had withdrawn from me emotionally because he had someone else with whom to share his thoughts and feelings. He no longer needed my support and encouragement. The pain of hearing him talk about her was almost too much to bear. In the morning, he told me that he still did love me. He promised he would call Melinda and end everything. He wasn't too convincing, but I wanted to hold onto this hope. . . so I believed him.

I decided not to tell anyone what was happening in my life and marriage except for my friends, Carol and Donna. No one else needed to know, especially since Mike promised to end the affair. I was also too embarrassed to tell people that my husband had cheated on me. After all, I was the one who taught other women how to be a good wife and partner. I blamed myself for his affair and felt that somehow I had failed Mike as his wife.

A few days later, I became emotionally paralyzed when the reality of the situation set in and I realized how close I had been or still was to losing my marriage. I became extremely depressed. For a short time, I even felt suicidal.

In my typically impatient fashion, I wanted us to restore our marriage and move on. We decided to seek help from a counselor. I found a male counselor that I felt would relate well with Mike. Mike went a few times, but his heart wasn't in it. One minute he would say he was trying, then he would say it was hopeless. He wasn't sorry and didn't seem to think that what he had done was wrong. At this point I didn't care; I just wanted things to be "normal" again.

Because of our impending move to Lodi, we had a home built in Stockton, a city near Lodi. It was our dream home in the country on three acres. In November, the house was completed. We weren't planning on moving until June, but we did take over a few things so we could stay there on weekends. Mike also moved over his belongings that he'd taken to the corporate apartment in Lodi. Once again he said he needed space and suggested that he move into our new house. His excuse was that he needed to be in Lodi for work. I questioned whether Melinda was still out of the picture, but I went along with his plan.

I began to read a Christian book about the male mid-life crisis. The authors advised a wife to leave her husband alone if he was struggling between her and his girlfriend. They recommended that the wife go on with her own life and not ask her husband a lot of questions about his life. So that's what I tried to do. He stayed at the new house and came home to San Jose once in a while to visit. The kids interpreted all the confusion as part of the impending move. We weren't working on the marriage, but we did go on a few of Mike's business trips together. We went to Hawaii and Carmel, California, both romantic locations where we could have worked on restoring our love. Instead, Mike remained distant. I continued to live in denial to protect myself. I wanted to believe that he still loved me and was just confused. I kept telling myself everything was going to be all right.

In December, we went to my parents' 50th anniversary in New York State. My mom had just recovered from a stroke and was out of the hospital. The day after my arrival, she had another stroke. She was unresponsive and the doctor said there was nothing more he could do for her. She was so ill that we felt she wouldn't make it through the night.

In the middle of this chaos, Mike arrived in Buffalo via a business trip to Detroit. Because of my doubts, I looked in his briefcase and found a Christmas card from Melinda. She wrote in the card that she couldn't wait until they could be together *forever*. What a shock! Then another card, this one from her son saying how glad he was that his mom had such a great man in her life. I wondered if he knew that Mike was married, had a family, and that he went back and forth between us and his mother.

I confronted Mike, and he told me he was planning to leave me right after Christmas. I was numb. My mom was dying and my husband was leaving me. I couldn't take any more. I told him just to leave and go to her, but he wouldn't because he didn't want to "spoil" the holidays for the kids. That was the worst night of my life.

My mom did live through the night, but she was very ill. I spent the rest of the week like a robot caring for her and the family. I was in shock, and didn't say anything about what was going on in my life. Everyone thought my distress was caused by my mom's condition. At the end of the week, Mike again said that he didn't want to leave after all, and that he would end the affair.

So in January of 1991, Mike took me to Reno to celebrate our 22nd anniversary. We actually had a good time and my hope was beginning to be restored.

Soon after our trip, I had to go back to Buffalo to help my dad with my mom. Mike had begun to spend more time in San Jose with the family, which I felt was a good sign. But when I called from Buffalo, he seemed distant and noncommittal again. I returned home as soon as I could, but Mike announced that he was going to be spending more time at the new house. He said he felt trapped and just needed to be alone. I was concerned that he was seeing Melinda again, but I followed the advice I'd been reading and gave him his space. No questions asked. As ridiculous as it sounds, I was willing to try anything. He lived in Stockton while we stayed in San Jose. The kids and I would go to visit him once in a while.

During these months, I struggled as a full-time student at San Jose State. At times I found it almost impossible to concentrate on my work. I felt like my whole world was crumbling around me, and yet I had to write papers and study. As I look back, it was probably good for me because it was a diversion from the crazy life I was living.

Mike came home on Valentine's day. He acted rather cold and only gave me a card, but I was glad to see him. The next morning was a Saturday and he announced that he was going back to Stockton to play golf. He had made his appearance for the kids' sake and was out the door. I felt resentful as he walked out and left me painting the inside of our house, getting it ready to put on the market.

Sunday night was one of the rare times that I called him. There was no answer. I was about to forget it when I felt God speak to my heart. His still small voice said, "Call Bally's Reno and ask for Mike."

I thought, "Why would he be there?" I did not know that he was heavily into gambling. I fought the urge, but then it came back even stronger. In my bewilderment, I obeyed and called. To my amazement, he *was* there. When they rang his room, no one answered. I knew he would not be there alone. Melinda had to be back in the picture. I thought, "This may be my only chance to confront them together."

In spite of what several Christian authors said about not forcing your husband to choose between you and the girlfriend, I drove to Reno to get his decision. I needed closure to this mess.

When I got there, I had the hotel page Mike. Needless to say, he was shocked as he entered the lobby and saw me standing there. His face turned an interesting gray color. At first he denied that Melinda was there, but eventually he pointed her out to me. I approached her as she sat in the restaurant. I told her that Mike and I were not separated or divorced, no matter what he had told her. I explained how he was going back and forth between us. She was speechless and just got up and strutted off.

I told Mike I wanted him to be honest with me and just tell me what he wanted. He nervously paced up and down the casino lobby and finally said, "It's you I love." He left with me that night leaving Melinda in their room. I have no idea what lie he told her. All the way home, he told me this should prove to me that he loved me, not Melinda. I so badly wanted to believe him this time.

February slowly passed. When Mike came home, he spent his time watching television and playing Nintendo. It was quite evident that he didn't want much to do with his family.

He was in Stockton most of March and rarely came to see us in San Jose. I didn't know what was happening. He stopped traveling to Detroit, so I thought maybe he was finally over Melinda.

Mike stayed in Stockton all of April. During one of my many lonely nights, I woke up and felt God urging me to call Melinda at her home in Detroit. Months earlier, I had found her phone number, but had never called it. I fought the urging for a moment and then remembered what had happened in February, so I called. A recording said the number had been disconnected. I waited a few hours and then called her work number. The woman who answered said Melinda had quit and moved to California. Again I was in shock, wishing this whole nightmare would end. I didn't think I could take much more. Little did I know what still lay ahead.

The next morning I called Mike at his office in Lodi and questioned him about Melinda. He denied that she had moved to California. Finally, when he knew I had the facts, he admitted that she had come to Sacramento, but he said it was against his wishes. I decided then and there the marriage was over. I was going to drive to Lodi and tell him. The kids were still in the dark about everything. Jennifer stood in the kitchen in a state of confusion as I got ready to leave. I was so upset that I told her what had been going with her dad. She didn't seem too surprised. I told her that I couldn't take any more.

On the ride to Lodi, I thought about why I had been fighting so hard for my marriage. Mike had been the only man in my life, and I had made a commitment to him. I valued my marriage, at least what it used to be. I could see in Mike all the signs of a distraught mid-life man, and I felt that one day he would come out of his crisis. I wanted to be there when he did.

After all, he had been there for me when I went through that rough first year of menopause. I was also afraid of being alone. But most of all, we were Christians. Shouldn't we be able to conquer this, rekindle our love, forgive and move on?

I remembered reading somewhere that during the mid-life years, many couples fall out of love. If they work at it, they can fall back in love and have a much stronger marriage than ever before. That's what I wanted . . . that's why I fought.

So by the time I saw Mike, I was again confused about what to do. Then when we talked, he told me he too was confused and didn't know what he wanted. He asked me to please give him more time. Once again, I decided the future of my marriage was worth the wait. I did ask him to spend time alone away from Melinda and me and to sort out his feelings and make a decision.

In May, the kids and I went to Stockton to celebrate Mother's Day and my birthday. It seemed as if Mike was still seeing Melinda. All day he paced the house and tried to get us to go home. I felt certain he had made plans with her and we were just in the way. Jennifer wasn't feeling well so we didn't leave until evening and Mike was angry. After all, it was my day with my family. I still hadn't told the boys anything except that their dad was going through a rough mid-life crisis. By now, I was good at covering and lying for him.

In May, I graduated from San Jose State, and Don graduated from the eighth grade. The first weekend in June, we had planned to move to Stockton. Suddenly Mike started talking about the kids and me staying in San Jose and not moving at all. I began to ask God for direction. In my quiet time one morning, I read Psalm 37:3-9.

Trust in the Lord and do good; *live in the land* and be safe. Seek your happiness in the Lord, and he will give you your heart's desire.

Give yourself to the Lord; trust in him, and he will help you; he will make your righteousness shine like the noonday sun.

Be patient and wait for the Lord to act; don't be worried about those who prosper or those who succeed in their evil plans.

Don't give in to worry or anger; it only leads to trouble.
Those who trust in the Lord *will possess the land,*
but the wicked will be driven out.

As I prayed, I felt that God wanted me to possess the land and move to Stockton. He did not want me to lie down and continue to give in to Mike's demands. I knew I needed to take a stand, so I told Mike that Don and I were moving to Stockton. Jennifer and Richard would stay in San Jose to finish school. I also made it clear that if Melinda was in his life, he could not live in the new house with us. I would not knowingly be part of a triangle. I think he was stunned by my assertive behavior, but he agreed he'd move out if he was seeing her. So in June, I hired the movers and Don and I went to live in our new home. Mike told me the affair was over, so he lived with us until July when I found out that he was still seeing Melinda. I insisted he move out and he did—right into her apartment. He lied and told everyone he was living in the corporate apartment. Even he was ashamed of his lifestyle.

On several occasions when Mike came to the house to get Don, he asked me to keep the home fires burning until his return. He told me he was planning to get out of his relationship with Melinda, and I wanted to believe him. He was very convincing, so I continued my wait.

I tried to keep myself busy. I continued reading books on the male mid-life crisis. The authors' advice was to wait, pray and work on improving myself. So for another three months, that's what I did. I tried to leave him alone. That was especially hard, because when he came to see Don, he would use his key and walk into the house as if he still lived there. Then he would go through my mail and snoop around looking at my calendar and phone index. I felt angry and violated every time it happened.

Mike also had control over all the money. He gave me the amount he thought I needed, and told me how to run the house and family. I became more and more resentful and told him to either get rid of Melinda and come home or just leave me alone.

Consequently, Mike came over one August evening and told me Melinda was out of his life. He told me his plans were to come home immediately. I agreed, but what I really wanted was for him to stay at the corporate apartment and take things slowly with me.

It wasn't very long after he was home that he became angry and resentful towards me. He said I had "forced" him to end the relationship, that he wasn't ready, and that he missed Melinda.

September, October, and November seemed endless. Mike was extremely unpredictable. He continued to be angry and pine over Melinda and did nothing to regain my trust or rebuild our marriage. My hopes were crushed, but I hung in there. Because of the way he was treating me, I was pretty sure he was seeing her again.

Thanksgiving weekend, the weather was cold and rainy, but Mike wanted to golf every day. I had the feeling that he was hoping I wouldn't go with him so that he could take off to see Melinda. I was determined not to let that happen, so I went and trudged through the wind, rain and cold. Mike was critical of the way I played, showed me no respect, and would take off, leaving me trailing far behind.

After Thanksgiving, I began to notice that his closet was again emptying. He'd take his shirts and suits to the cleaners and never bring them home. He was leaving them at work. This was one of those "subtle" signs he was up to something.

In December, he took me to the company Christmas party and paraded me around, making sure everyone saw us together. He was being very lovable. I could tell it was all an act, but I wasn't sure what others thought.

The next morning he announced he was going hunting "alone" for the rest of the weekend. My protests did no good, so I gave up. I believed Melinda was going with him, but I needed proof before I could confront him. On Saturday I called her apartment and, of course, there was no answer. I called again Sunday evening and she answered. Now I was sure that Mike was there too, so I drove to her apartment. I saw his car parked out front. I immediately went to the door and knocked. Mike answered and yelled, "What are *you* doing here?" I couldn't believe his nerve. I told him to come home and get his things.

It was over an hour before he pulled into the driveway. He stomped into the house and said he was tired and that we would talk in the morning. He proceeded to get ready to go to bed, in our bed. I was furious and told him to get out of the bedroom. He slept in the guest room. The next morning, he left and moved in with Melinda again.

In mid-December, I began to dread the coming holidays. Mike came over on Christmas day and brought presents for all of us. The boys wondered why their dad didn't stay for dinner.

From December to July, we rarely saw Mike. In January, he called and wanted to celebrate our 23rd anniversary. I told him there was nothing to celebrate. He came by the house a couple of times each month to take Don to dinner and a movie. Once in awhile, he asked me to join them. I was now busy with my own life. I had new friends and activities and had become active in my new community. All this had helped me not to focus on Mike and what he was doing.

Still, no one but Jennifer, Carol and Donna knew what was really going on. It wasn't too hard to keep the secret from my parents, since they lived so far away. I avoided old friends and just told them that Mike was on the road a lot. We both let people think we were still living together.

In June, Jennifer got married in Monterey and we both went to the wedding. Mike was extremely affectionate and told me that he wanted to get back together. He said he was trying to figure out a way to dump Melinda. I was excited to be with him. I thought my prayers were finally being answered.

On July 2nd, I took Jennifer and Don out for dinner. We happened to pass Mike and Melinda on the road. Don recognized the car and yelled to me. Then he saw the woman by his dad's side. He panicked, thinking I knew nothing about her. I could see his angry face in the rear view mirror. I told him I knew about his father and Melinda. He said through his tears that he had wondered if his dad had been cheating on me. All the craziness of the past years began to make sense to him. That night, I was the one who had to deal with Don and all his emotions over his dad's deceit.

Mike came over the next day to see us. I told him Don had seen him and Melinda. He was noticeably upset because now his son knew about all his lies. He paced the yard for hours and finally decided not to go home to Melinda. He stayed the night in the guest room. Melinda must have driven by and seen his car at our house. She immediately returned all of his belongings and planned to go home to Detroit. Mike had the nerve to ask me if we could give Melinda $5,000 so she could move. I was happy to get rid of her, so I agreed. It was worth $5,000 to get her out of our lives.

Again, Mike wanted to come home immediately. I wanted him to stay in the corporate apartment so we could reconcile slowly. He said he wanted to come right home because he couldn't stand being alone. How ironic, since he had been telling me for years what he needed was to be alone. In reality, he was never alone.

For a while I was excited. I thought we had finally made it. Melinda was gone and we were together. In the first weeks, Mike seemed to be trying. Before long, I realized he was only trying in front of others. When we were alone, he was verbally and mentally abusive. He would sarcastically put me down and ridicule me about my looks, intelligence and abilities. He told me that he wanted to be accountable to me and earn back my trust. So, when he traveled, he'd tell me where he would be staying and that he wanted me to call him there. Several times this happened and when I would call, I'd find he wasn't even registered at the hotel. When he got home and I questioned him about it, he'd rant and rave about how I was never going to trust him again.

Once more, his clothes began to disappear from our closet. I would see him looking through rental magazines for apartments. If I said anything or questioned him about the magazines, he would laugh at me. Every time I got into his car, he turned off his car phone. When I asked why, he said Melinda could still be trying to reach him. So I wondered why turn it off only when I am there? There were times when I felt I was going crazy. This time, things were worse than they had ever been. In front of the kids, he acted loving, but when we were alone, he turned on me.

My folks visited in September and my dad sensed something was wrong. Mike's behavior was odd. When my dad went to Mike's office with him, he saw all of Mike's clothes in his office closet. My dad was perplexed, but had no idea of the hell I had been living.

In October, Mike took a business trip and called one night to tell me he wasn't happy with the way our lives were going. He said he wanted to move into the guest room when he got home. I agreed, since I had wanted a slow reconciliation anyway. But instead, the day he arrived home from his trip, he packed his car and waited outside for me to get home. When I arrived home and saw the blank expression on his face, I knew he was leaving. In my heart, I knew this was the last time for us both. He said it had nothing to do with Melinda. She was gone . . . out of his life for good. He just needed his own apartment, and maybe someday we could try dating. As he pulled out of the driveway and my life, I broke down. All of the chaos of the last years was for nothing, all hope was gone, the marriage was over. He had made his choice.

I realized that, in his coming home, we were all living a lie. He was trying to convince the kids that he was working hard on the marriage, while in reality, all along he'd had someone looking for an apartment for him and Melinda. She was never out of the picture, only back in Detroit living on our $5,000 until he could get free of me.

A few days later, we met with our kids to inform them that dad was gone again. They were tired of hearing it. For the first time, we told Richard about Melinda. He was hurt and very angry. I realized I should have told him when Don found out. Mike kept emphasizing that Melinda had nothing to do with his decision to leave. He told the kids that she was gone and that he was living alone. He wanted them to believe this so in the future they would not hold it against her. That's what this last time was all about, convincing everyone he had tried.

I cried as I watched our family fall apart, knowing I could do nothing to stop it.

A few weeks later, Jennifer called her dad at his apartment rather than at work. Melinda answered the phone. Now we knew they *were* together. He was caught again.

CHAPTER THREE
Alone and Waiting

This chapter focuses on the months I spent alone while Mike went back and forth between Melinda and me. I had decided to wait. It was my choice. At the time, I really didn't comprehend how hard it would be to live with my decision.

If you should find yourself alone and waiting, realize that this will probably be one of the most difficult times in your life. If you are like me, you'll want to know how long you'll have to wait and what the final outcome will be. Unfortunately, there is no way to predict what will happen. Each situation is unique and only God knows how it will end.

The waiting period is a confusing time as you sort through your emotions and needs. I felt like a fish out of water, uncomfortable even in familiar situations. I didn't know where I fit or belonged. If you make the decision to wait, prepare yourself for what lies ahead. It isn't easy. You may feel **single**, but you are not. You may not feel **married**, but you are.

During this time, it is imperative that you maintain an active, fulfilling life, which is easier said than done when your whole world is falling apart. I didn't feel much like being sociable, but I pushed myself to get out.

I cycled through all the states of grief over and over again. I had gotten over the shock, but the depression, loneliness, distress and panic would cycle back and forth.

I was often preoccupied with worry and stress and had a

hard time concentrating on tasks. I could forget the simplest thought or message. Don was often frustrated with me, but it was understandable since he was unaware of all that I was going through. I also had a difficult time sleeping. When I would wake up in the middle of the night, it was so awful to realize I was alone. As my thoughts wandered, I'd find myself panicking with the prospect of growing old alone. When I did sleep, I would often dream of having no money and having to live on the streets. I looked to my counselor for help whenever I could get to San Jose, but it wasn't often enough.

I considered getting help from a psychiatrist so, if necessary, I could be given antidepressants. But after thinking about it, I decided I didn't want to take medications that would really just postpone my having to deal with the situation. I felt that for me it would be best just to endure the emotions and pain and move forward. Every one of us is different, and we have to decide for ourselves what course of action to take.

When I first discovered the affair, I was a senior at San Jose State University. I managed to finish school and graduate with a B.A. in Clinical Psychology. I had a difficult time concentrating on my studies, but I am grateful I was committed to finishing.

I had the idea that getting my own life together while I waited would help me overcome my anxiety and panic. In order to do that, I searched for "safe" activities. I stayed away from groups and functions which included a lot of interaction with men—especially single men. While you are waiting to see what is going to happen in your marriage, it is best to limit your time around men who will give you the attention you so desperately crave. Male attention can help ease the devastating feelings of rejection. So be careful, remember that you made the decision to wait.

One way I began to put my own life together was by developing new women friends. I acquired a new circle of friends who did not know me during my life with Mike. When I moved to Stockton, I became a Mary Kay beauty consultant. I loved going to the weekly unit meetings, special events, conferences, and our grand extravaganza in Dallas every year. It was all great fun and a wonderful diversion. The other consultants were warm, friendly, and anxious to be successful. Just the kind of women I needed to be around.

I also became a volunteer at the local Women's Center several days a week, counseling abused women. I facilitated two weekly support groups and counseled the residents at the shelter. I enjoyed working with both the clients and other counselors.

These involvements kept me busy and made life easier while I waited. They also gave my life purpose and fulfillment.

Besides using this time to develop new friends, it is a good idea to work at building better relationships with old friends. I now know that I should have been honest with my friends about what I was going through. Friends can be a valuable source of fun, encouragement, and support.

Whatever you decide to do, it is important to stay busy. It is best not to dwell on your husband and his behaviors.

Since Carol and Donna knew what was going on in my life, I enjoyed being with them. I could be myself and be open about my feelings, fears, and thoughts. As my prayer partner, Donna gave me immediate access to her whenever I called. The first months, we talked daily. When I was in Lodi, I often showed up on Carol's doorstep in tears. She was never too busy to listen and pray with me. I really appreciated how she would get right where I was emotionally. Whether I was sad, angry or fearful, she was there with me. I don't know how I would have made it through that time without Donna and Carol. It is important to have at least one person with whom you can talk and cry openly and honestly.

My daughter, Jennifer, would rush to my side whenever a

new crisis erupted. During this time, she had married and given birth to her daughter, Amy. They both brought a tremendous healing to my life. I was comforted when I held and cuddled my little granddaughter. Jennifer and Amy's frequent visits were the highlight of my week. Jennifer and I developed a special closeness that has grown over the years.

I wanted to be around people while I waited. Some women choose to isolate themselves. Although alone time is necessary, total isolation during a crisis is unwise. Depression can creep up and engulf you before you know what's happening.

When I was alone, I read. I particularly liked studying Christian self-help and mid-life crisis books. At the time I was going through my crisis, I couldn't find a book written by a Christian woman who had experienced the pain and abandonment of adultery, and who had come through it better, not bitter.

In addition to my quiet time reading, I found solace in gardening and yard work. I loved the sunshine and fresh air. The time I spent outdoors was peaceful and gave me the opportunity to think and reflect on my life.

I also began to develop many new interests. In addition to pursuing my new Mary Kay career and counseling, I took golf lessons. I hadn't realized how much I would enjoy golf. I also began to explore my new community. I attended plays, concerts and museums with friends. I even bought my very first dog. Max's companionship was especially comforting during this time.

I had other fun adventures such as trips to visit friends and family and vacation getaways. I flew to Buffalo and loved spending time with my parents, even though it was hard not to tell them what was actually going on in my life.

Throughout this difficult time, I added many new dimensions to my life and in the process grew. If you do all this and your husband should come home, it will be exciting for him to get to know the "new" you. You will have a lot of experiences to share with him.

I also continued to have my quiet time with God every day. That's where I gained the strength to wait. There were times that I felt God must have forgotten me and that He wasn't aware of what I was going through. Then I would run to get my Bible, and He would let me know that He still cared very much. He did understand the frustration of waiting and being alone. Some scriptures that brought me comfort were:

Psalm 1:6– For the Lord watches over all the plans and paths of Godly men.

Psalm 4:8b– For though I am *alone*, O Lord, you will keep me safe.

Psalm 37:34– *Don't be impatient* for the Lord to act! Keep traveling steadily along this pathway and in due season, He will honor you with every blessing.

The Living Bible

Many of my devotionals encouraged me to continue in my wait. God was working on my impatient attitudes and I finally gave in and trusted him. Listed below are a few of my daily readings.

"We must *learn to wait*. When we do not know what to do, we must simply do nothing."

"*Wait* till the fog clears away."

"God had not given me any direction yet so I *waited*."

"*Waiting is a great part of life's discipline* and therefore, God often exercises the grace of waiting in the anxious hurrying person." (Me)

"The Father cares when He sees his children in the teeth of a

31

blinding storm, but he knows that *faith grows in the tempest*. He will hold our hands bidding us not to try to see the next step to take."

"We should not move in uncertainty. *If we are not sure, let us be quiet and wait!*"

These scriptures and devotions gave me a peace when I just wanted to run away and leave Mike.

As impatient as I have been all through my life, only God could give me the ability to wait. I wanted closure. Now I am glad I waited and gave Mike every possible chance to return to his family. This way I don't have regrets that I acted too soon.

Waiting was not easy, but having God to turn to gave me strength. Many of the authors who advocated waiting stressed not setting deadlines or pushing for a choice between you and the other woman. That may be fine for a while, but only you know when you are breaking and your tolerance is gone.

During your time of waiting, your husband may want to come and go out of your life. If he is living with another woman, you should set boundaries. He needs to know what you expect from him and what is not acceptable. I made some mistakes during this time.

I regret that I allowed Mike to enter my home with his key when he came to pick up Don. By his choice, it was no longer his home.

The last time Mike said it was over and wanted to return home, I should have set boundaries on what I felt was acceptable. Dr. Les Carter, in his book, *The Prodigal Spouse*, states that, "If inconsistencies are allowed during reconciliation, they only create a lack of respect toward the injured mate. It is an act of responsibility for the injured mate to continue restoration **only** as fidelity is maintained."

It became extremely important for me to protect myself. Eventually I learned that if I discovered Melinda was still in

Mike's life, any reconciliation on my part ceased.

If your situation ends well and your husband gives up his girlfriend and comes home to you, great. You made it that far. You will still have work to do, but the hardest part is over. At least you will be working on the marriage together.

But should your situation go as mine did and your husband leaves you for the other woman, you should have no regrets. If you spent your waiting time wisely, you will be well on your way in your new life as a single woman.

CHAPTER FOUR
Suddenly Single

The waiting is over, and you know that he will not be coming home again. Now what?

When Mike walked out the door the last time, I knew it was for good. I knew he had no intention of returning and I was to the point where I couldn't take any more of his emotional and mental abuse. I felt less of a person each time he came home and left again. It was time for me to let go.

It was also time to break the secrecy. We had a family meeting and told Richard, as Jennifer and Don already knew about Melinda. I began to tell our friends, starting with Ron and Joyce. Ron was not surprised; he had suspected it for a long time. Joyce was shocked and angry. When I told my parents, my dad was upset and concerned about me. My dad had loved Mike and had treated him like his son. I knew he was disappointed in his actions. My mom didn't say much, but since her stroke, she has shown little emotion. Friends that I hadn't seen for two years were absolutely stunned. Many of my female friends were uncomfortable with the whole situation. They worried that if this could happen to me, it could also happen to them.

I wanted Mike to be the one who would file for the divorce. In fact, I pleaded with him to do it. He refused. I couldn't understand why at the time, but it soon became clear. Since we had done nothing about filing legal papers, he still had control of all the money. He knew everything would be equally divided in a divorce, and he was in no hurry to be forced to share anything with me. He liked being able to give me what he decided and not what the courts said I deserved. He also said he had no intention of marrying Melinda. So, from his viewpoint, his life was much better if we kept it this way.

When I knew it was over, I needed to put the whole mess behind me. I needed closure. I wanted to be released from the nightmare I had been living.

I decided I should begin by finding a good attorney. Mike suggested that I use his lawyer, thinking it would be cheaper to share one attorney. He tried to convince me that in sharing an attorney, there would be more money left for *me*. I refused, knowing that the attorney's priority client would be Mike. The attorney would not consider what was best for me. Then Mike gave me a list of lawyers whom he knew and recommended, hoping that I would use one of them. Fortunately, I found my own attorney, one who had an excellent reputation. Needless to say, Mike was enraged and I was convinced that I had made the right choice.

It was hard for me to sign the papers that would end my 24-year marriage. I resented that Mike hadn't finished what he had started. I even had a few pangs of guilt because deep inside, I believed divorce was wrong.

I talked to a singles' Pastor at a local church, hoping to get some measure of understanding and sympathy. Instead, I got a big **why**? The Pastor asked me why I was filing for divorce. He thought that I should continue to pray and wait, no matter how long it took. I tried to explain to him that I couldn't take any more, and that Mike had no intention of returning home. I felt judged, criticized and condemned. I was already a victim and this pastor made me the victim a second time.

As soon as I could, I talked with Pastor Ron. I knew he would give me an honest Biblical response. He assured me that

Mike had divorced me earlier by starting and continuing his adultery. Ron said I was just cleaning up Mike's mess and doing the paperwork. I experienced a sense of relief being supported and not chastised.

Going through a divorce is one of the most traumatizing experiences of a lifetime. Since I had been alone and waiting for a long time, I thought that would make the divorce easier. But the finality of it all hit me. I felt a tremendous loss and rejection. At times, I thought it would have been better if Mike had died. I experienced the whole cycle of grief over and over. Just as I thought I was doing better, another wave of emotion would hit me.

Certain times during the day and certain events triggered the most sadness for me. For example, the dinner hour and Sunday afternoons were particularly difficult. It was best to break the old routines and develop new ones. I began to fix dinner earlier, and would then go out to the store until dinner time was over. I changed the pattern of my Sundays by being with friends or going to lunch with my Sunday school class.

I forced myself to face the reality that I would soon be "legally" single. Previously, I had thought that I could face anything as long as Mike was by my side. Now I was forced to face my life "alone." I was very grateful that I had already begun to develop my own life and activities.

I was fortunate that I could take the needed time to heal without feeling the immediate pressure to work and earn my own living. I was receiving more than satisfactory alimony and child support. Many women have no choice but to work as they go through their divorces. If you didn't have a career during your marriage, you shouldn't rush out too soon and take just any job. It is really important to take your time and decide what type of career interests you. You may need to get more schooling. Many times the court will rule that your ex-husband take care of you while you get your education. Discuss your options with an attorney, not your ex-husband, or you may jump into something that you later regret.

My children were a wonderful source of enjoyment. Since they were older, they were also great encouragers and supporters. Only Don was left at home and we grew very close. I did all the things with him that a *father* should do. I taught him how to drive, went to his school events, and took him back east with me to visit my parents and to see the Baseball Hall of Fame. Richard, as the eldest son, was concerned for my well-being and I knew I could always count on him. He helped me make decisions and offered his advice. However, I did not want my children, especially my boys, to feel responsible to have to take their father's place in my life. Jennifer and Amy continued to visit frequently. We bonded as females and had fun together. They came over from San Jose regularly for visits and one fall, I took them both to Buffalo to visit my folks. Our holidays, which could have been sad times, were actually wonderful as our family gathered to celebrate.

I decided to join a divorce recovery group. I searched for one that would meet my needs, and I went on a regular basis. Each week, we would listen to a speaker, and then we would divide up into small support groups. It was especially helpful for me to listen to the men in the group. Several of them had wives who had been unfaithful, and their pain was just like mine. Listening to them helped me not to focus on adultery as strictly a male issue.

Again, being with friends helped me to reconstruct my life. I became close with Linda, another Mary Kay consultant, whose husband had recently died. We immediately bonded to help each other in our grief. I must admit I appreciated having a friend who was also suffering the loss of a mate. It really didn't seem to matter if it was through death or divorce. She understood the turmoil and loneliness I was going through. Since we were both alone, we spent lots of time together or on the phone talking for hours. Many weekends she stayed at my house. We'd go to a movie or just hang out. We spent several holidays together. She and her daughter joined Richard, Don, and me for Christmas Eve. We played games and drove around looking at the decorated houses.

One summer adventure which Linda and I pursued was camping at a nearby lake. It was exciting, even though we really weren't sure what we were doing. We managed to get the tent up by ourselves. We even rented a speed boat and zoomed all over the lake. We felt an exhilarating sense of accomplishment.

Together we joined "Parents Without Partners." We attended the coffees and discussions and an occasional dance. During this time of transition for us both, we experimented with different groups and activities. We also began to line dance, which was quite a challenge. I began to attend line dance lessons several times a week. It was great exercise and, best of all, I didn't need a partner. I was really impressed that I could actually remember so many of the dances.

Then one day Linda made a great discovery when she happened into a local coffee shop. She met Debby, the owner, and immediately bonded with her. Debby is fun, outspoken, and a wonderful listener. I began to stop in for coffee every day and often wound up staying for hours. Debby became a good friend. She took the time to introduce me to her other customers. I made numerous friends and contacts while I sat there. The coffee house became more than just a place to hang out; it was more like a support group.

Eventually, I tried another church singles' group, and was pleasantly surprised at the support and understanding of this pastor. I felt comfortable in the group. I wasn't ready to be involved in ministry. I just needed to rest and revive my relationship with God. I went to Sunday school, but found attending the church service was too painful. When I saw all the happy families, memories of what my life had once been were triggered. Even going to the singles' class was a struggle, but I knew I needed interaction with other Christians. Ron and Joyce had moved to Lodi and started a new church, but I could not yet attend there because Mike and I had shared their dream and vision. I continued to hang onto God; I knew he had been holding onto me.

I enjoyed many of the activities of the singles' group, including lunch out on Sunday afternoons, super bowl parties, picnics, and monthly pinochle games. These events gave me a full social calendar. I liked being busy. I became good friends with many of the women in the group. I found that I also enjoyed being around men again. I was not ready to date, but it was nice to enjoy male company.

It took my divorce one year to be final. Mike and I struggled over money, property, and other issues. I was surprised at the amount of child support and alimony I was granted. God was taking care of me. I also received half of Mike's retirement account, which I rolled over into my own investment account. One of my biggest fears had been for my financial security, and with that issue settled, I found it much easier to move on.

Being single does not mean that life is over for you. Hopefully, you'll be able to see that you can have a whole new beginning. If you can motivate yourself, you can get involved in all sorts of activities and ministries. Ministry to others especially helps lighten your load and gives you victory, purpose, and hope.

CHAPTER FIVE
Personalities and The Role They Play

Your personality plays a major role in the way you will handle an unfaithful mate. It is extremely helpful to know and understand why you do what you do during this time. Also, discovering your partner's personality will help you understand some of the underlying reasons he chose this destructive path.

God created you as a unique person with your own individual personality traits. But each of us also falls into at least one of the four basic categories of personality temperaments which Hippocrates named: Choleric, Sanguine, Phlegmatic, and Melancholic.

Learning about your personality temperament is not only informative, but can actually be fun as you begin to understand yourself and gain insight into your behavior. The book, *Your Personality Tree*, by Florence Littauer, has a simple test to help you determine your temperament type. In her book, Florence describes the strengths and weaknesses of all four of the types. Right away, I recognized that Mike's temperament was that of a Choleric. She describes the Choleric as a born leader with a tremendous ability to motivate others. She lists the strengths of a Choleric as adventurous, persuasive, forceful, daring, independent, and productive. Some of their weaknesses are: unsympathetic, workaholic, domineering, manipulative, and short tempered. Cholerics want to be in control.

They tend to have an angry, hostile side, but can also be very charming. They quickly get bored and move on to new endeavors. This description seemed to be written with Mike in mind.

Another personality test is the Myers-Briggs. A short version of this test is included in the book, *Please Understand Me* (Character & Temperament Type), by David Keirsey and Marilyn Bates. Without getting too detailed, I will explain the letter abbreviations used to score the test. Your test score can be any of the many combinations of these letters, but only one letter from each of the four groups. The groups are: I/E, S/N, T/F, P/J. The I/E represents introvert vs. extrovert. People who are introverts (I) are usually energized by being alone. They like to be around people, but the interaction easily tires them out. They tend to be possessive and territorial about their environment and property. In contrast, an extrovert (E) is energized by people. They are social and feel lonely when apart from others. The N/S represents intuitive/sensation. People who are intuitive (N) are very much the dreamers of the world and they tend to live in their fantasies. They have great speculation about their future and what it holds for them. One problem they encounter is that if they ignore reality too long, they end up out of touch with the real world. People who score high in sensation (S) are very practical and grounded in reality. They trust facts and actual experience. Unfortunately, they may not see all the possibilities in their future. The T/F group represents thinkers vs. feelers. Thinkers (T) are frequently male. They make their decisions on the basis of principles. They believe strongly in policy, laws and justice. Thinkers are often thought by others to be cold and heartless. On the other hand, feelers (F) are very often female. They make their decisions on the basis of personal impact. They believe in social values, sympathy, devotion and harmony. They are often thought to be too soft-hearted, illogical and emotional. The last group is the J/P which stands for judging vs. perceiving. People who score high in judging (J) are those who like deadlines, closure and planning ahead. They are often thought by others to be rigid and inflexible, whereas those scoring high in perceiving (P) are very flexible, tentative and like to let life just happen. They resist deadlines and closure. They are often thought by others to be indecisive and aimless.

After you take and score your test, you can then read about the characteristics of your personality combination. It is an eye-opening experience.

As I read the book, *Please Understand Me*, I became convinced that Mike would score as an ESTP. According to Keirsey and Bates, the ESTP is a person of action who makes life come alive. "They like to work close to the edge of disaster." At times, they are ruthless. "If their desire for excitement is not met constructively, however, these energies may be channeled into destructive antisocial activities."

The authors describe ESTP personalities as living in the now, bringing unpredictability into their relationships. Their relationships tend to be conditional depending on what they have to gain from them. They seek excitement through risks. "They are always seeking the thrill of courting Lady Luck in one fashion or another (gambling, etc.)."

When I read these books, I was amazed at how accurately they described Mike's positive, as well as negative, side. It gave me a clearer picture of the man I had lived with all those years.

Tim LaHaye in his book, *Understanding the Male Temperament*, also has much to say about character and personality types. He states, "What we do is a result of who we are, our character is who we are when no one else is around." Tim says a hostile and self-centered man will become aggressive and, in most cases, lawless. He will disrespect the laws of both God and man. That statement explains a lot.

When Mike was living for Christ, all of these weak areas in his life were under the control of the Holy Spirit. He used his leadership skills and his ability to motivate others at church and in our family. He sought his thrills in acceptable, healthy ways. When he decided to go his own way, his weak, human character took over. He became a candidate for seeking his thrills outside our marriage.

Learning this helped me to see why he was so vulnerable to adultery. He liked adventure, excitement and living on the edge. He was willing to take risks even if it meant losing his family. The comfortable home life we had been experiencing became boring, and he went for the temporary thrill.

Men have affairs for many different reasons. They usually occur more out of the desire for thrills and adventure than out of the need for sexual fulfillment. In Mike's case, I feel adultery was not only due to his character, personality and temperament, but also due to his age and fast-paced business career. I really believe this combination made him a susceptible candidate for an affair.

He was 40 years old, approaching mid-life. Because we married young, I think he was afraid he'd missed some of life's excitement. During the time he went back and forth between Melinda and me, he often told me that he was bored and felt trapped.

As for his career, he moved quickly up the corporate ladder and found himself in a position he had never dreamed possible. He traveled frequently and had many opportunities to indulge his fantasies. I've heard stores about people who gain success quickly, beyond even their own expectations, and then fall prey to feelings of superiority and the thought that they deserve more from life. They often become immoral and unethical.

I feel Mike's decision to cheat involved many dynamics. Over the years, I've come to realize this was within him and really had little to do with me.

After gaining so much insight into Mike's personality, I was anxious to find out more about me, so I took the personality test in *Your Personality Tree,* by Florence Littauer. I wasn't surprised to discover that I was a Phlegmatic/Sanguine. Learning this helped me to understand why I handled this situation the way I did. Florence lists the Phlegmatic's strengths as: adaptable, peaceful, submissive, controlled, obliging and tolerant. The weaknesses include: fear, indecision, nonchalance and reluctance.

Phlegmatics have also been described as insecure, self-protective, loyal, and needing close relationships. This was an accurate description of me.

When I read all these traits, I better understood why I waited so long, always hoping that Mike would come home. It also helped clarify my fears, pain, and frustrations. Loyalty is a major part of my personality, so I stuck by him no matter what he did or how he treated me. In extreme loyalty, I lied and covered for him. I had him on a pedestal and truly idealized him as a husband. My marriage was an extremely important part of my life. Because I tend to be insecure, I needed Mike to love me and I needed to be number one in his life. At the end, I was constantly frustrated because I wasn't even a top priority. Another reason I had fought his leaving was out of my fear of being alone.

On this test, I also scored high in the Sanguine categories. Some of the Sanguine strengths are: talkative, emotional, innocent, and living in the present. Weaknesses include: an expectation to always have fun, restless energy, naiveté, and allowing circumstances to be in control. Sanguines are also scatterbrained and in need of attention and approval. I find it hard to admit, but that's me.

As a Sanguine, I am emotional and talkative, so I experienced Mike's aloof attitude toward me as extremely painful. I do like to enjoy life and want to experience pleasure in everything I do. I understand that I need to learn to accept the hard times when life isn't "fun."

My naiveté kept me believing Mike, even when he was blatantly lying. Often, I had let my circumstances control what I thought and how I acted.

My friends and family know that I tend to be a bit of a scatterbrain. As I mentioned earlier, all through our dating and marriage, I had done one crazy thing after another. Mike had never seemed to be too bothered by it until this time in his life when he had someone else and could now be critical of me. He no longer thought my antics were cute or funny.

I also took the Myers-Briggs Personality Test and discovered I was an ESFJ. In the book, *Please Understand Me*, ESFJs are described as people who promote harmony, idealize those they admire and are energized by people. They do not want to be alone. ESFJs love to entertain and socialize. They need to be loved and appreciated. They have a strong sense of values and expect others to abide by them. They want closure in their decisions. Again, this accurately described me.

I definitely wanted harmony in my marriage. I needed Mike to love and appreciate me, and I felt rejection when he no longer did so. ESFJs need closure to important issues and I was frustrated that we could not resolve this mess.

I liked learning about the various personalities. I now have a much better understanding of people and I am more tolerant of others' differences. I also acquired needed insight about myself.

I have discussed only Mike's and my personality types. I didn't mention anything about the melancholic or the other letter combinations of the Myers-Briggs Test. If you would like to learn about all the temperaments and types, I would recommend that you read any of the books I mentioned.

Remember that no personality trait is set in concrete. If you are aware of your weak areas, you can ask God to help you change. God is always working on and in us to mold us into His image.

CHAPTER SIX
Is Adultery Abuse?

Abuse is defined as a corrupt practice or custom, a deceitful act, to maltreat, injure or damage. Abuse can appear in any of the following forms: verbal, mental, emotional, sexual, or physical.

Verbal abuse involves threats, put-downs, sarcasm, and name calling. Mental abuse involves actions that are meant to intimidate another person. Yelling, smashing and throwing objects, and driving recklessly are all forms of mental abuse. Emotional abuse is classified as a form of manipulation, denial, withdrawal, isolation, or any behavior meant to control another. Sexual abuse occurs when one person forces another person to perform a sexual act against his/her will. Physical abuse is anything which is done against another person that causes physical bodily harm, such as: pushing, hitting, slapping, biting, kicking, punching, choking, hair pulling, or the use of a weapon.

Abuse of any kind is wrong. It is **never** justified or deserved. Victims often believe that the abuse is their fault. They need to be told over and over that they are not to blame. What if the woman is, as her partner often claims, lazy, mouthy, or fat? Does that mean she deserves to be punched, kicked, choked, verbally threatened, or killed? The abuser has the right to leave the relationship, but never to abuse his partner.

In our culture, boys are often raised to be aggressive. Violence has been more or less a tolerated behavior for males. We seem to believe that anger is an acceptable male emotion, while crying and the expression of feelings such as sadness and loneliness are wimpy, not macho. Young men are taught that to be a success at work or home means to have power and control.

Girls are often raised to be "feeling" oriented. When girls cry, we see it as a good release. They are trained not to show anger and are rewarded for their passive behavior. Thus, we end up with a society of angry, yelling men, and passive, crying women. As we begin to re-educate and encourage our young men to discuss and release feelings, and also to understand that angry, controlling behavior is unacceptable, violence in relationships may begin to decrease.

It is time our society began to recognize ALL forms of abuse, including adultery. Cheating on a partner is sexual, as well as physical, emotional and mental abuse. It is the height of dishonor and disrespect. The words "affair," "fling," "playing around," and "infidelity" sound rather innocent. But nothing is innocent about adultery. It can ruin lives, leaving a marriage and family devastated. One "little slip" can start a landslide which wreaks havoc on everyone even remotely involved.

I believe it is time for us all to take responsibility for our actions and stop condoning a culture that blames anyone or everyone for our problems. We blame our parents, siblings, teachers, mates, religion, society, and even God. Rarely do we hear someone say, "I was wrong; it was my fault."

If the man committing adultery is a Christian, he becomes a hindrance to the cause of Christ unless he repents and turns his life around. If he continues as if he's done nothing, he affects his children, family, friends, and all the non-Christians who are watching him.

Unfortunately, our society does not view adultery as abuse. At times, it is even encouraged with such phrases as, "Every man needs a little variety in his life," or "A little fling may spark up your marriage," or, "He deserves it." Mothers have even told daughters not to make a big deal of adultery as long as her husband comes home at night. Movies glamorize the act of adultery and turn it into a romantic story.

Once you have been the partner of an adulterer, you have a different viewpoint on the innocence of the act.

There are many books on the shelves today boasting of ways to affair-proof your marriage. Yes, you can and should work at your marriage, but you cannot affair-proof it. The problem with the idea that you can affair-proof your marriage is that it says you are responsible for and can control another person's behavior. That is a lie. If you buy into it, you live with a false hope that if you do everything just right, your mate won't ever cheat on you or leave you. It is time to see that adulterers are responsible for their own actions. Please let's **stop** blaming the victims by saying they could have prevented it by acting differently or by being a better spouse.

Men cheat for many reasons. Their personalities and life experiences all contribute to this decision. Yes, it is a decision. It just does not happen without some thought. A man may feel trapped and long for freedom. Whatever his so-called reasons, he has the right to leave the relationship, but he *never* has the right to be abusive (unfaithful). Men can choose to be committed and loyal and work on the problems, or leave the marriage.

When I say they have the right to leave, I am aware that, as Christians, we do not see divorce as an acceptable option. However, it is certainly better than ruining the lives of spouses and children through abuse or adultery. Unfortunately, many people, including Christians, make the choice to have an affair rather than work at the relationship or get a divorce. When other people hear about a man's adultery, they say things like "I wonder what she did or didn't do? Did she get fat? Was she frigid?" Even other women fall into this line of thinking. I think it makes them feel safer to blame the victim. That way they can believe that if they perform correctly and look good, their man will never leave them. There are some women who have a superior attitude toward divorced women; after all, they still have their husbands.

Please don't hear me wrong. We should constantly strive to be women of God and to be all that God expects us to be as partners.

The bottom line is that even if you do strive to be the model wife, your husband may still be unfaithful. We women shouldn't live in fear of what our husbands may one day do, but we should be all that God wants us to be today and trust Him with tomorrow's outcome.

Unfortunately, many of us have been abused some time during our life, whether as a child, youth, or adult. Abuse is one of the major causes of low self-esteem. It is no wonder that many women suffer from low self-esteem. A brief definition of self-esteem is the reputation that you have with yourself or the confidence you have in your ability to cope with life's challenges, to be successful, and to assert your needs.

Your self-esteem or, in other words, the way you see yourself, affects the kinds of friends you select, the jobs you take, and your view of the world.

One of the most devastating events that can happen to lower self-esteem is the rejection by a spouse. Divorce is often worse than the death of a spouse because you not only deal with loss but with rejection. Consequently, during and after a divorce, it is important to recognize and work on developing your self-worth or self-esteem.

When you have poor self-esteem, you find it almost impossible to act in your own best interest. As you begin to know and value yourself, you will be less likely to become involved in an abusive relationship. The main focus of your life will not be to find another man.

Good self-esteem can be the result of feeling physically and emotionally safe, along with having a sense of belonging. Emotional safety is being able to share your thoughts, dreams, ideas, and feelings with someone who will value and respect you. It is important to know that you can say what you want without it being used against you. Your self-esteem is enhanced when you feel safe, secure, and accepted. Most of us have a desire to be loved and to feel that we belong to someone. We have the need to bond with other people. This need for close ties to others is especially important in times of severe stress or crisis.

These needs can be met in many ways. It is important not to expect to get them met solely in a relationship with a man. It is best to join organizations, support groups, church groups, and to begin to build a network of supportive friends during this time. It is helpful to surround yourself with people who will accept and love you. Being part of a group helps you to develop your capabilities and feel valued and understood. We all need to give and receive love, and that can be done with your friends and family.

Feeling good about yourself is not only accomplished by belonging and feeling safe, but by accepting yourself where you are today. We all need improvement, but that will come later. As you set goals and follow through with decisions and projects, you will begin to feel better about yourself. You may want to keep a list of ten qualities you like about yourself; refer to it when your mind replays the negative words people have said to you over the years. Read books about self-worth to help you work through this area.

Lastly, but most importantly of all, you can boost your self-esteem by knowing and believing you are valuable to God. He created you. He died for you. He wants to live within you.

That makes you special. Don't measure your worth by the world's standards: physical beauty, money, or IQ. God looks at the inner man. The important qualities are: kindness, love, peace, patience, integrity, trust, and honesty. These are all areas that you can work to develop.

If you can believe that God, knowing all your faults, loves you anyway, then maybe you can also learn to love yourself.

CHAPTER SEVEN
Just Who Am I Really?

After the initial turmoil and craziness subsided and I settled into single life, I began to question what "I" was all about. I asked myself, *"Who am I, really?"*

I first became aware of my confusion when I attended a local singles' function, and the people there asked me questions about myself. I discovered that I had difficulty responding. Much of what I had to say was more about Mike or about Mike and me as a couple. I was 45 years old and had somehow let the years go by without developing a real sense of "me"— my own identity.

I believe we all have two identities: One is our external identity which primarily consists of our roles in life, the other our internal identity which is made up of our needs, interests, ideas, beliefs, attitudes, and personality. My external identity was very closely tied to my family. I was not only a wife and mom, but also a volunteer at school, in little league, and at church. Since Mike was a church leader, I was often accepted more as an extension of him and his ministry than as a leader in my own right.

However, there were times during my marriage that I did have my own external identity or roles that weren't connected to Mike or the kids. I was an Area Coordinator for Friendship Bible Coffees in San Jose, and in that position, I set up home studies throughout the city. In later years, I returned to college and had my own external identity as a student at San Jose State University. As a college student, I enjoyed it when the younger students viewed me as just another classmate. They talked with me about their personal lives and problems. They knew nothing of my life off campus and did not know that I was a mother with kids their age. In fact, when Jennifer and Richard also became students at State, I resented somewhat their intrusion into my new world. I felt a little guilty for not wanting to acknowledge my own kids, but I also feared my new identity would once again become tied to them. I was excited about having a new environment in which to define a new external identity for myself.

I found that examining my roles (past and present) was an important part of finding out who I am today. Many of my past roles are gone. My primary and favorite role as an adult had been as a wife. I had found it very fulfilling.

My secondary role was that of a mother . . . another position I loved and found fulfilling. Now with my youngest off to college, I know I am still a mom, but no longer "mothering." The loss of those two important roles left a huge hole in my life.

My role as a daughter has also faced major changes as my parents have aged. They now live in Lodi and I find myself looking after them. Our roles have switched, as I now feel and act more like the parent.

My role as a friend experienced changes as I went through my divorce. Friends have a more significant role in my life than they had when I was married. I have developed a supportive circle of woman friends and would find life difficult without them.

Over the years, I have added a few new roles to my life. Five years ago, I became a grandma for the first time. This is one of my favorite roles.

Dating again and being a "girlfriend" is another new role. I thought it would be a hard one for me to accept. I hadn't been on a "date" for more than 25 years. Three years ago, I met Phil at line dancing lessons. We got to know one another and then began to date. We have had a wonderful time together. After really knowing and loving only one man, I find this an unusual experience. I'd forgotten the excitement in dating and getting to know that someone special. Phil is a doctor, a psychiatrist, so we share an interest in psychology and counseling. It has been wonderful to find out that I could be so very much in love again.

So my roles changed, forcing my external identity to change, but there is one role that will remain constant, no matter what happens. I will forever be a child of God.

As I spent time "alone and waiting" and as a new single, I encountered my own identity crisis. Due to my changing external identity, I was forced to rethink who I was internally. What were my needs, ideas, beliefs, and interests? I wasn't sure anymore. Since Mike and I had married at such a young age, I had overly attached and adapted myself to him. In doing so, I had lost sight of myself.

In thinking about my marriage, I could see that it was very co-dependent. Co-dependency is one of the buzz words of our generation. Many people don't fully understand just what it means. If you dissect the word, it makes more sense. *Co* means joint or equally, while *dependent* means to rely on or to be addicted to someone or something. Mike and I were equally addicted or overly attached to one another. It makes for a dysfunctional relationship, but that's how many of us started out. For years, we women have been raised to believe that the right man would come along and meet **all** our needs. We believed that "Prince Charming" would ride into our life and rescue and care for us forever. That's exactly why we have been so willing to give ourselves totally to our man. After a while, we both become so enmeshed that it's almost impossible to know where one person ends and the other begins. In a relationship such as this, the woman often ends up never developing her own internal identity.

I believe that to prevent this kind of entanglement, we should all have boundaries. When we are young, we don't seem to know enough to set boundaries. We often want the closeness that merging ourselves together into one brings about. Webster's Dictionary defines a boundary as "something that fixes a limit or extent." Setting boundaries is hard and sometimes frightening, even when our motive is only to protect ourselves.

Boundaries help you to establish what behaviors you will accept or tolerate from others. You may feel some guilt about protecting yourself, and may think that you are just being self-ish. You may be confused as to what to do if your boundaries aren't respected. You may also discover that people who have no boundaries themselves, find it hard to respect the bound-aries of others. If you don't know and understand yourself, you will find it almost impossible to set your own boundaries. Your confusion about boundaries appears to give free reign to others that they can treat you as they wish. This can then lead to abuse in a relationship.

Because there are few, if any, boundaries in a co-dependent relationship, the two people are overly entangled. When one person in the couple decides to leave the union, the separation is extremely painful for the one remaining. The pain can be alleviated quickly by reconnecting to your partner or by finding another person with whom to connect. Unfortunately, many people are too eager to attach to someone right away, and don't go through the discomfort of the separation. Ideally, it is best just to feel the pain and give yourself plenty of time to heal naturally. During this time, it is important to take the focus off being in a relationship. Find out what interests you, try new things, meet new people, and learn to make your own decisions.

In my marriage, I had let Mike make most of the major decisions. I had not resisted his choices even though I didn't always agree. I wanted harmony in our home, so I went along.

Making my own decisions was a part of learning about myself. I was interested to see the process that I went through each time I was faced with a major decision.

After the divorce, I was immediately faced with buying my own home. Mike and Melinda had moved into our Stockton home and Don and I needed to find a place for us. I started praying for God's guidance and He began answering me. I was introduced to my Realtor in the coffee shop one morning, and two days later, I put an offer on a house. The price, location, and size were right and the house was just what I wanted. Everyone to whom I showed it gave me positive feedback, and I knew it was the right choice. I got input from others, but the final decision rested with me. I felt so good being in charge for a change.

The next major purchase I faced was buying a car. This was actually scarier than purchasing a home. As a single woman in a car dealership, I felt like a minnow among sharks. I finally decided on a small sporty car . . . no more family station wagons and vans.

I knew that as I began to acquire my own things, I would need a will. I found an attorney and drew up a living trust. I was taking care of business and I felt great.

For the first time, these were my decisions . . . good or bad. I was taking responsibility and in doing so was becoming more self-assured. I was changing and I liked what I was learning and discovering about myself.

Your individual needs are also part of your internal identity. There are certain needs that are basic to each of us. Learning to acknowledge and understand these needs is important. Acknowledging your needs and being needy are two different things. A needy person is someone who is looking for that one person to satisfy all their needs. Instead, look for fulfillment from your family, friends, jobs, clubs and organizations, yourself, and, most importantly, from God. He knows and understands you.

You have both psychological as well as physical needs. God created you with the need to belong, to be accepted, and to receive approval and love. When these needs are met, you begin to feel safe and content and are then more able to help meet the needs of others. When you experience a loss in your life, your psychological needs may go unmet. You can then become resentful, disillusioned and bitter. How you experience and deal with loss can give you insight into yourself. Loss in life is inevitable. It can be very painful, but the result is often personal growth.

Over the past years, I've suffered many losses. In the loss of my husband and marriage, I lost most of my future dreams and plans. Living alone, I daily feel the loss of family routines. Through all of this, I have learned to let go of those I love, if necessary. I have learned that life changes, and that change can be good. I now know that it is not good to rely solely on any one person. I must rely on God. People may leave me, but God will always be there. I can count on Him for He knows my every need.

If you really want to discover and get to know who you are, use the tools that are available to you. I have already mentioned the importance of personality tests and self-help books. Time alone is essential to discovering more about yourself. If you were to meet someone whom you desired to know better, you would want to spend quality time alone with them. Well, the same is true when you want to get to know yourself. You need to have time to be by yourself. In the past few years, I have spent a lot of quality time alone. Many of the books which I read helped me think about my life, where I have been, and where I want to go. I read my Bible and prayed for God's guidance. His wisdom has given me a clearer picture of who I am on the inside. I do not just fill roles. I do have my own identity which consists of my personality and all the distinguishing characteristics which set me apart from others.

Use this time to write down your thoughts, feelings, and even your dreams. Writing about yourself in a journal helps you to focus on your internal thoughts and feelings. A journal can be used as a tool to lead you through the healing process.

Trying to decipher your dreams may give you a clearer picture of yourself also. God may even choose to speak to you through a dream. Be sensitive and pay attention to your dreams. They are usually about people, places, and things that are very important to you. It is not always easy to figure out the meaning of a dream, but I think you will find it worth trying.

I think that emotions are a window through which you can see what is going on inside. They are your responses to the circumstances of life. Emotions are never right or wrong, they just are.

Over the years, your internal and external identities change. Change is good, as it leads you to discover new aspects of yourself. That's what growth is all about!

Discovering who you are is an important tool in being able to move forward, set goals, and most importantly understand and love yourself.

The bottom line is that no one knows you better than God. As you spend time in Bible study and prayer, He will show you who you are, and who He wants you to become. As you look to Him for direction and wisdom, He will begin to clarify and define your identity.

CHAPTER EIGHT
Am I There Yet?

You may be wondering what the other side of adultery and divorce is like or how you will know when you have finally arrived. Getting to the other side can be an extremely complex process requiring more time than you may expect. Questions will arise as you contemplate your situation and where you are in the whole process. You may ask yourself: **Is it wrong to be angry? Is being able to forgive necessary for healing? How will I know when I have really let go and moved on? Will I ever be able to trust a man again? When will I stop thinking about the past and what we had and the future and what I thought it would hold? Will I ever get to the other side of it all?**

Let's look at these questions one at a time. First of all, is it wrong to feel anger? The answer is no. Anger is a natural response when your rights have been violated, your boundaries disrespected, when you've been lied to and deceived, or when a commitment is broken. All of these things have occurred in a marriage torn by adultery. Another underlying cause of your anger may also be fear. You may be afraid to lose your partner, your security, or even your purpose in life.

Anger can be good, as it motivates you to make necessary changes in your life. Problems don't occur just because you're angry; they occur when your anger is not handled properly. The Bible says you can be angry and sin not. When you feel anger, it is important to try to discern what caused the anger. Are you angry with your husband, the other woman, or with God?

I experienced anger at all three. I did manage to work through my anger with God by finally coming to terms with the fact that Mike was created with a free will. God does not take away our choices and force any of us to be obedient to Him. I knew that what had happened was not God's intention or fault. I was able to realize that my anger was really not with God, but more with Mike and Melinda.

The anger that I felt toward both of them fluctuated from week to week. I felt violated and rejected. After Mike left the last time, my anger began to surface. I felt used and worthless. I was confused and wondered, "Just who is the real Mike?" Was he the man I had been married to all those years, or was this person who had now come forth the "real" one? Had our whole life together been one big lie? Had he deceived me all along? I was upset and angry.

I learned ways to cope with my anger. Exercise, long hot baths, and lots of talking helped. Having a counselor with whom I could honestly share my feelings and anger was also a tremendous help. Instead of acting out my anger with revenge or retaliation, I used it as a motivating force to move on with my own life and to grow spiritually and emotionally. Dealing with my anger forced me to read books about anger and drove me into the Bible seeking God's guidance.

I felt that becoming a successful person in my own right would bring me satisfaction and help alleviate my anger. I also found that taking charge of my life and being in control of myself gave me the freedom to let go of any resentment. When a woman is manipulated and controlled in her relationship, she usually experiences anger. Seeing that I could take control of my life gave me the power to set boundaries with Mike. To finally set boundaries with Mike felt exhilarating. I had decided that after the divorce, I did not want to have contact with either Mike or Melinda. I needed to protect myself, so I never gave him my telephone number. I got a post office box to which he could send my monthly check, and kept my home address a secret. I dealt with my anger by taking care of myself and helping others. I had accidentally discovered assertiveness and it felt great.

Given enough time, your anger will begin to dissipate on its own. Time is healing.

In *The Anger Workbook*, by Dr. Les Carter and Dr. Frank Minirth, the authors describe five ways to deal with anger. They discuss suppression, denial, aggression, assertiveness, or just dropping it.

They state that the first three forms (suppression, denial, and aggression) are "self-serving and only manage to perpetuate the anger." Suppression and denial don't really accomplish anything and manage to keep the anger alive. Aggressive anger is turned on others and doesn't care about anyone else. It is usually abusive and blaming.

But when you deal with your anger in an assertive manner, you feel more powerful and in control of yourself. You can care for yourself while still being considerate of others. They also mention the validity of establishing boundaries as an important protection mechanism. When your boundary is violated, you have the right to stop the person, but you don't have the right to be aggressive or abusive. According to Minirth and Carter, dealing with your anger by being assertive is healthy and healing.

Last of all, there are times when you can simply choose to drop your anger. You decide that nothing will be accomplished by holding onto it. This is not suppression, but realizing you are angry and then letting go of it. It is not easy, but it is possible if you ask God to help you. The Bible says in Ephesians 4:31, 32 that problems and attitudes such as bitterness, anger, and malice can be replaced with kindness.

Anger can be used in a positive way to get you to make changes in your life. It also gives you the freedom to say, "That's enough, no more." If you concentrate on assertive anger or dropping anger, it *is* possible to be angry and sin not.

Forgiveness is another important issue. Is healing possible without it? What if your spouse isn't sorry and hasn't asked for your forgiveness? Forgiveness is much harder, if not impossible, if you are still going through all the ups and downs of the pain and anger. Don't rush. Let yourself go through the healing process one step at a time.

According to Webster's Dictionary, healing means to restore health, to mend, to patch up a breach, to return to a sound state. Forgiveness is not denial, acting as if nothing has happened. It is acknowledging the pain, but deciding to give up resentment, a claim to a requital, or to give relief from payment (pardon).

Can you heal and be restored to emotional health if you hang onto resentment and continue to wait for payment? I believe if you want to return to a sound state of mind, you need **eventually** to pardon or forgive. Forgiveness is not done so much for the other person, but for yourself.

Forgiveness doesn't mean you are completely over the hurt and pain of the betrayal and loss. But somewhere in the whole process, you make the choice to remain hurt and wounded or to heal and move on. It really is your choice. No one can make you forgive another person. To be honest, most of us like to hang onto our hurt and resentment. It seems to bring us comfort. Hopefully, you will decide to look ahead to your future and will release the past. I believe part of the release includes forgiving.

Too often, forgiveness is forced. It is something to work toward, but not to force or fake. When I first discovered Mike's adultery, I immediately forgave him and just wanted it to end.

I believed he had made a mistake, so I was willing to forgive. It was premature. I had to forgive every time he came home. He hadn't said he was sorry or even stopped the deception.

Forgiveness is still possible even if the offender never admits, stops, or is sorry for the adultery. According to Dr. Les Carter, the author of *The Prodigal Spouse*, "Forgiveness can be understood as a matter of initiative rather than the result of another's show of repentance." Injured spouses can choose to forgive because unforgiveness brings unfruitful emotions for them.

Some people feel reconciliation should be the outcome of forgiveness. I don't agree. I think you can forgive whether the other person accepts it, rejects it, wants a relationship or not. You may forgive and yet decide that you do not want a relationship or any contact at all with the other person. Whether you have contact or not doesn't really matter. God knows your heart.

Forgiveness can't be earned but just given freely. You deserve not to be weighed down with the burden of an unforgiving spirit. It poisons you, **not** the adulterer. He made his choice and will suffer his own consequences. You are responsible for yourself and your choices.

God is there to help you gain complete healing. If you think you can't forgive, ask God for help. He will guide you to a point where you have a willingness to forgive. Then He can take your willing heart and bring you to the point of forgiveness, health and healing. Psalm 147:3 says, "He heals the broken hearted and binds up their wounds."

When you can finally come to terms with forgiveness, the situation or person no longer has power over you.

I don't think it is possible to let go and move on without first handling your anger and coming to a point of forgiveness. Letting go means releasing your past, your marriage, your spouse, as well as your future and what should have been. It is over whether you want it to be or not. Letting go means facing what lies ahead without holding onto all the securities of the past. It means not *denying* but *accepting* your life.

Don't expect to let go overnight. The longer you were married, the longer it takes to release the hurt and pain. Try not to get down on yourself when those old thoughts and emotions from the past creep up on you. Be kind to yourself and give yourself all the time you need.

Moving on means planning a different life, a future without your spouse. Just keep looking ahead. Set goals and have a plan for your future. This is your chance to start all over. At one time, you may have thought you could not have a life without him, but you will ultimately see that you can. Make it a good one! Your mate just went from one relationship to another, nothing really that different. You have all kinds of options open. Take the time to look at them all. Hopefully, there's no rush to make such an important decision. You may want to return to school, start or change a career, and eventually one day remarry. Look at all of this as one of life's challenges, not disasters. Romans 8:28 says, "That all things work together for good, to those that love God and are called according to His purpose." God is in charge. You may be surprised to discover that your life actually turns out much better.

You'll know when you are moving on because the past will not hold you back. You'll be through hoping that maybe you'll get back together. You will have your own life and wouldn't even consider taking him back. You will be making healthy decisions for you and your children. You will be able to see old friends without bursting into tears. You won't live in your memories. You will no longer think about him and wonder what he is doing.

Being able to let go gave me new energy and excitement in my life. I feel better about myself and I'm finally realizing my potential. Don't be shocked when you do have a setback. They are inevitable, but try not to let them hold you back from your move forward toward healing.

I have temporary setbacks when I let myself focus on my fears. Fears can paralyze us, whether we fear not making it financially or being alone. I have learned not to dwell on these thoughts. God doesn't want us to live in fear, but to trust Him for our daily provisions and companionship.

In the past, I experienced setbacks when I heard gossip or news about Mike. When he married Melinda, I felt hurt and betrayed again. I felt his replacement of me was now complete, and that he had wiped away all of our years together. When I would hear about their life together, I would feel very depressed. I have come a long way and am finally beyond caring what goes on in their lives. As you develop your own life, you will care less about his.

Your husband's actions may have made it difficult for you to trust people. You may feel that your friends let you down. If they continued to socialize with your husband and his girl-friend, you probably felt betrayed. As for trusting another man, that may take some time. When you begin to socialize, look for male friends who have integrity, honesty and loyalty. It isn't good to be too eager; take your time and test each situation. Keep in mind that not all men are alike and if you ever want to have a loving relationship, learning to trust a man will be necessary. If you allow yourself to think that no man is trustworthy, you will end up being hurt more than anyone else.

Don't be in too big a hurry to fill the emptiness in your life with a man. You have other things to deal with first. Realistically, you should be well on your way to forgiving, letting go, and moving on before you involve another person in your life. You should also be socially active, emotionally stable, well aware of your weaknesses and fears, and in the process of working on them. It is not a good idea to date when you are still feeling desperate or needy. Feeling comfortable by yourself is important.

Until you can find some measure of victory in these areas (anger, forgiveness, trust, and letting go), you aren't ready to date. If you do, you will probably experience disaster.

When you are in a new relationship, give yourself the freedom to have your own opinions, thoughts and feelings. Don't enmesh yourself totally into his life. Don't be swept off your feet with flowers and romance, but look realistically at the qualities of the person. If the qualities you value and want in a person aren't there, don't continue to date that particular man. Middle-aged adults often think their time is running out and they have to settle for whoever comes along. Don't fall prey to that deception. Be choosy. You deserve it. Stay alert and don't overlook behaviors that are red flags.

Watch his behavior for signs of addictions, abuse, temper, and possessiveness. How does he talk about other women, including his mother? Does he always see women at fault and say derogatory comments about them? Does he blame others for his problems? Does he ridicule or humiliate you? Does he want to know where you are and what you are doing all of the time? Has he decided he doesn't like your family and friends or that they aren't good enough to you? Does he frequently lose his temper and take it out on you? Do you walk on eggshells trying to please him? Does he find your kids an annoyance? If you answered yes to these questions, **watch out**, you are headed for trouble again. Instead, look for someone who treats you with respect and honors your rights and decisions.

Keep in mind that, given enough time, whether you are involved in another relationship or not, you will eventually get to the other side of adultery and divorce.

You will know you are there when you have let go of the past and all that you and your husband had together, and

70

when you have even let go of the future and all the wonderful times that you planned on having together. On the other side, you will see that life is again fun, exciting, and purposeful. Your thoughts will no longer be centered around you and your problems; you will be able to focus on the concerns of other people. You will want to reach out and minister to other women.

You will not only be on the path to forgiveness, trust, and moving on, but you will be able to see your situation as an opportunity for growth, not as just a disaster. You will even find yourself looking forward with hope and anticipation to what God has planned for the years ahead. Today you are beginning **your** future. With God's help, go and make the very best of it.

Selected Bibliography

Carter, Dr. Les. *The Prodigal Spouse*. Nashville: Thomas Nelson Publishing, 1990.

Carter, Dr. Les, and Minirth, Frank. *The Anger Workbook*. Nashville: Thomas Nelson Publishing, 1993.

Keirsey, David, and Marilyn Bates. *Please Understand Me*. Del Mar, Ca.: Prometheus Nemesis Book Company, 1984.

LaHaye, Tim. *Understanding the Male Temperament*. Tappan, New Jersey: Fleming H. Revell Company, 1977.

Littauer, Florence. *Your Personality Tree*. Dallas: Word Publishing, 1986.